THE BLUE PIRAT

The sun shone in the sky
and the sky was a deep blue.

The sun shone on the sea
and the sea was a deep blue.

The red pirate sailed away
across the deep blue sea.

He sailed in his ship
away from the island.

The green pirate sailed away
across the deep blue sea.
He sailed in his ship
away from the island.

But the blue pirate
sailed back to the island.
He sailed back to the island in his ship,
to look for his boots.

He did not forget that he had left his boots on the island. He sailed back.

He left his ship
and went to look for his boots.

The island lay green and brown
in the sunshine.

And the grass was green;
the grass looked very green
in the sunshine.

There were flowers on the island.

There were red flowers

and blue flowers

(but there were no green flowers!).

There were yellow flowers

and white flowers and purple flowers.

And the sun shone on the flowers,
and the sun shone on the grass,
and the sun shone on the island,
and the sun shone on the sea.

The blue pirate looked for his boots.

He had no boots,
so he went on the grass,

and he went very softly.

He went this way,
and he went that way.
He looked this way,
and he looked that way —
and he saw the red pirate's hat!

The red pirate's hat
lay there on the grass.

"Ah!" said the blue pirate to himself.
"The red pirate must be
on the island."

He left the red pirate's hat
there on the grass
and went to look for his boots.

He went on the grass,
so he went very softly.
He went this way,
and he went that way.

He looked this way,
and he looked that way —
and he saw the green pirate's knife!

"Ah!" said the blue pirate to himself.
"The green pirate must be
on the island."

He left the green pirate's knife,
and he went on, across the grass.
He went on the grass,
and he went very softly.
His boots lay in the grass by a tree.
He saw his boots there in the grass.

The blue pirate sat down on the grass
and put on his boots.

Then he said to himself:
"The red pirate is on the island
and the green pirate is on the island.
I must get my gold and sail away.
I must sail away across the sea
and look for another island.
I will hide my gold
on another island."
So the blue pirate went
to look for his gold.

His gold was hidden in the sack,
and the sack was hidden
down under a tree.
The blue pirate looked for the tree.
The tree was by the sea
and there were blue flowers
and white flowers under the tree.

The sun shone down on the flowers.
The blue pirate saw the flowers
and then he saw the tree.

He looked in the tree,
and there was the sack.

The blue pirate took the sack
out of the tree.
He put the sack down on the grass.

He shook out the gold
and it lay on the grass.
It shone on the grass in the sunshine.

"Ah!" said the blue pirate.
"This is my gold."

Then the blue pirate put the gold
back in the sack,

and took the sack back to the ship.

He went back to the ship,
but he didn't go so softly.
He had his boots,
so he didn't go so very softly.

He put the sack on the ship.

He sat on his ship
and he looked at the island.
He sat on the ship
and he looked at the sea.

Then the blue pirate said to himself:
"Far away there is an island,
far away across the sea.
And the name of the island
is Acrooacree.
I will sail far away,
and look for Acrooacree."

So the blue pirate left the island,
and sailed far away across the sea,

and as he sailed he sang to himself.

He sang as he looked across the sea:

"I will sail away

For a year and a day

Across the deep blue sea.

I will sail away

For a year and a day

To find Acrooacree.

Acrooacree, Acrooacree,

Across the deep blue sea."

So the blue pirate left the island,
and he sailed away, far away,
to look for Acrooacree.

And as he sailed the sun went down,
and set in the sea.
The sky was red in the setting sun,
and the red in the sky
shone red in the sea.

And as he sailed far away,
the blue pirate sat on his ship
and looked at the sky.
He looked at the sky
and he looked at the sea.
"I will find the island,"
he said to himself,
"I will find Acrooacree."
And he sang to himself very softly.

Football is my game. I think I am not bad at it!

I play on the wing. I must run fast and keep up with the ball.

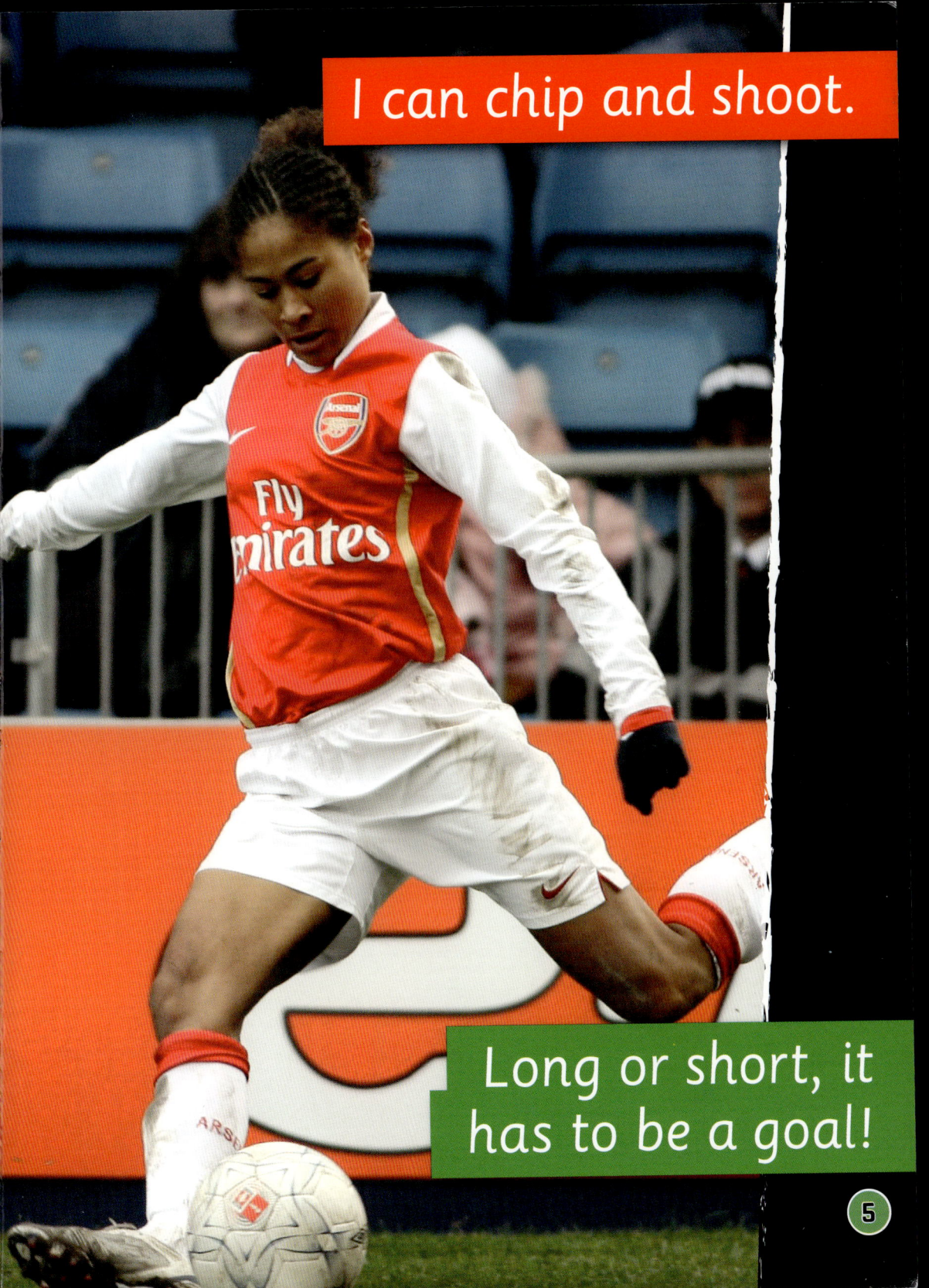

I can chip and shoot.

Long or short, it has to be a goal!

When I was 8 most football teams had just boys in them. So I hid the fact that I was a girl and played in a boy's team as 'Ray'.

But at one match I was seen by boys I knew. I had to admit I was a girl, and I was sent off the pitch!

I was banned from playing for the team!

It was a setback, but I had a lot of willpower and at 16 I was picked to play for Arsenal.

The team did well!

I get a buzz playing for all teams, but I get an extra buzz when I play for England. I have 80 caps so far!

Playing in the USA was such a buzz, too.

Now I am a coach as well as a player. I might train you one day!